Best Mom Ever Mother's Day Journal: The Perfect Gift Book For Mom
Mother's Day Gift Book: Thank You For Everything You Do. I Love You.
Paperback ISBN: 978-1-989733-33-2
Copyright Dunhill Clare Publishing 2020
All Rights Reserved. Cover Design by Sharon Purtill

www.ingramcontent.com/pod-product-compliance
Lightning Source LLC
Chambersburg PA
CBHW071719020426
42333CB00017B/2331